Anna L. J Arnold

Mozart

A Rhapsody

Anna L. J Arnold

Mozart
A Rhapsody

ISBN/EAN: 9783743332614

Manufactured in Europe, USA, Canada, Australia, Japa

Cover: Foto ©ninafisch / pixelio.de

Manufactured and distributed by brebook publishing software
(www.brebook.com)

Anna L. J Arnold

Mozart

MOZART.

A RHAPSODY,

. . . BY

ANNA L. J. ARNOLD.

✠ ✠ ✠ ✠

. DAYTON, OHIO. . .

1893.

WRITTEN FOR

MOZART CLUB, OF DAYTON, OHIO,

ON THE

CENTENARY OF MOZART'S DEATH,

DECEMBER 3, 1891.

MOZART.

The Temple doors of Sound
Swing open wide
Their gold-hinged noiseless valves.
With wooing throbs,
That almost rob
Volition of its power,
The pulsing fullness
Of the vibrant air,
From the great vault there,
Allures, with magic force,
The waiting soul
Into the whole
Great swelling sea within.
Then softly back they sweep:
And Care,
Despair,
And Grief, and Pain,
And thwarted Hopes,
And fevered Brain
Are left without their kind, embracing fold.

MOZART.

The Temple doors of Sound
Swing open wide
Their gold-hinged noiseless valves.
With wooing throbs,
That almost rob
Volition of its power,
The pulsing fullness
Of the vibrant air,
From the great vault there,
Allures, with magic force,
The waiting soul
Into the whole
Great swelling sea within.
Then softly back they sweep :
And Care,
Despair,
And Grief, and Pain,
And thwarted Hopes,
And fevered Brain
Are left without their kind, embracing fold.

'Tis Music's sacred court!
Who enter here?
Happy hearts, from far and near,
Seeking more cheer,
More beauty, more happiness to bless
Their earthly lot.
Broken hearts, torn with pain
And wrung with grief,
Seek a consolation brief,
From the Source Divine.
Homesick hearts, lonely here
For the friends so dear,
Longing, and weary, and praying
For heaven.
And, in the hallowed place
Each finds,
As Music winds
Her soothing spell,
That "All is well."
Cheer, blessing, solace, love and hope
Drop gently round them all,
As dewy fragrant twilights fall,
And shut away
The fretful day.

The flood of music wells
Out from some hidden source,
And gathers as it swells
Aloft, along its course,
Billow on billow strong
Of liquid song,—
Till the wild waves break
In foaming cadences of melody,
Against the far-off shore
Of heaven's bright crystal floor,
That backward flings the strain,
Re-echoing down the airy plain,
The subtle harmony,
That swells, recedes and dies,
Faint with its own great stress,
Its own rare power to bless,—
Then, lives anew,
Panting and sobbing, the great temple through.

The overture sweeps on.
Its clashing chords
Resound,
Rebound, and blend,

Until—at the end
They melt,
And sob themselves away
In pure, sweet harmony.

The prelude ends.
The sweet tone-painter sends
A rippling melody,
That floats
On the surface of the notes,
And it thrills,
As he wills,
Along the sentient nerves,
Responsive to his touch.
On the canvas of the air
Thus he limns, with prescient care,
Studies complete,
With power replete,
Enveloped around
With harmonious sound,
Like the golden apples rare
In the silver pictures fair,—
Till, *the senses change their realm,*

And the ear becomes the eye,
And his thoughts transparent lie
  On the vibrant warm background.
    True! Music is painting
      Done in sound.

    The theme is Life,—
Great, infinite, all-embracing life,
    Centered in God,
  But reaching out, out, out,
  Into the great abyss about
    The unknowing and unknown.
      Life!
    Forever rife,
With all of joy, with all of strife!
Wonderful, worshipful, terrible
      Life!
    Sublime the symphony!

    With majestic, stately sweep
  Flows on the swift, wide, deep
  Rush, of the music's matchless mysteries.
    Some stately octaves,—

A soft, sweet chord or two,—
Then, the bright strong movement thro',
Rippling triplets,
Sparkling runs,
Merry trills,
Chase, and leap, and bound in glee,
Creating for the fancy free
A limpid gladness, only found
In the "Heaven that lies around
Our infancy."
As the music gains its sway,
Out from the tissue of the tune
Into living day,
A tiny boy,
Not four years old,
Patters with baby footsteps bold,
And baby hands
Reach up to find,
Along the key-board ivory-lined,
The sweet, clear chords.
No words
His lips can form,
But, from the first,
The high fine soul

Must be heard;
And to the end,
He ever reaches up to find
The outlet
For the music in his mind.
At work, or play,
The livelong day,
'Twas music ever
That held the sway.
A father's wisdom, love and care
Are the firm chords there,
That bind, and hold,
In prescient fold,
Husbanding for richest life,
The youthful heart, with music rife.
Thro' the thrilling strains,
E'en from the first,
Is heard the wild glad burst
Of great applause,—
The favor that lifts
To courtly homes.
And, too, from the first,
Work! Steady work
E'en Genius may not shirk.

So blended in this strain,—
The sweet, bright tale
Of the bright child ways,—
Come, o'er and o'er again,
The cheery heart,
Touching common things to art,
Adulation, love, and work,
And the spirit's tender glow,
As the father's instincts show
The path that leads to Fame and God.
The boy heart lives,
The boy heart gives,
Thro' all the changing years,
Tho' success be far
And want be near,
A courage high
That knows not fear.

The harmony grows richer,
The great tone-artist flings,
As the delicate melody sings,
Into fine relief
Against the life-entangled maze

Of the youth's bright days,
The picture,—still more clear.
With soft euphonious charm,
The restless agitation,
In most delicate gradation,
Slides gentler, gentler down,
Till, with intensity profound,
There comes—a stillness, *redolent* with sound—
Some "murmuring, dying notes,
That fall as soft as snow in the sea,
And melt in the heart as instantly,"
While the music whispers
The old, old tale,
And love thrills out in a glad new birth,
As stars gleam forth o'er the dewy dark earth;
And the strains grow wild,
And the strains grow clear,
With the impassioned impulse
Of love's glad joy, and its anxious fear.
And the work?
Aye, the work!
For another's life, for another's cheer,
Hard ceaseless work, year after year,
To win the Rachel of his heart,—

Forever, now,
The music of their lives doth blend:
And to the end,
Melodious measure, firm, sustained,
With power to bless, tho' hope has waned,
In their love contained
The essence pure of harmony divine.
Aye! *Comfort the heart*,
If a great grand part
In unison must be maintained,
That Genius may, forsooth,
Purity, Unity, Truth,
Blend in the firmament of Art.

The mingled perplexity,
The tumultuous power,
Of the firm crescendo
That flings a shower
Of sounding chords out on the air,
Tell—the endless endurance and grace:
Tell—the high ideal,
The tame hard real,
The earth-clogged dragging pace,

Which Success doth make,
When she will o'ertake
Who struggles toward her fane.
And the music throbs, and pants,
In sympathetic touch
With the spirit that aspires,
And hopes, and strives for such
A wealth of freedom and of peace;
That born again, to life and light,
Triumphant in its God-given right,
Untrammeled by sorrow, want, or care,
It may, unchecked, its good gifts share.

Irresistibly impelled
By the melodies that welled
Forever in his brain,
To the work that he *must* do,
To serve to Art most true,
Nor live in vain,
Thro' the music's swirl,
His heart doth hurl
To himself, this precious pearl.
"Be true, O be true!

What tho' the soul must wait?
Achieve. Be true,—*and wait*,
Trust in thy God, and laugh at Fate."
And the echo comes back faint:
"Do. True.
Wait. Fate."

The great rugged beauty of the strain,
As the harmony swells out again
Thro' all the parts,
Like the spell that holds in dreams,
Till is heard, it almost seems,
The beating of the hearts,
Pictures, as it waves
Away, and laves
The spirit in soft airs,
With graphic tints of tone,
The man to Master grown.
The same sweet phrases there:
The sister in the heart,—
The father's guiding care,—
The same courageous cheer,—
The working without fear

Of the result,—
And, ever with the rest,
The reaching up to find,
As did the baby mind,
The Highest and the Best.
And thus, with ever growing stress,
With cadences that press
Along the sounding heights
Of the trembling, vibrant flights,
The experiences of life
Repeat, renew
And strew
The melody with sweeter power.
And it gathers, as it flows,
All the ecstacy that grows
In the spirit self-subdued,
With that perfect peace imbued,
From loyalty to God,
And loyalty to Art.
Till, at last, triumphant measure
Proclaims "Success!"—the treasure
Sought,
And bought
With the nerve force,

And the life-blood,
And the wild heart beat
That wrenched it
From the clutches of Defeat.
At last !
Exultant ! Fervent !
With dignity and grace,
Flowing on with stately pace,
With trumpet peals
That half reveal
The pageantry and glare,
And drum beat, and aria sweet,
And choral antiphony,
With thunder's crash,
And cymbals clash,
The music tells of *Victory.*
The canvas gleams with light :
Day is evoked from night ;
And ladies fair, and gallants brave,
And lords and ladies, fair and grave,
And Emperor, and royal train,
Musicians, singers, and the people, too,
Crowd in the picture's radiant hue,
And add a rythmic glad delight,

To the clear *sounds* that greet the *sight*.
The *Master* sways the wand.
Responsive to its gleaming beat
Such fancies float, so wild, so sweet,
They haste "the waiting soul to meet,"
And hold it victor, ere it knows
From what the magic influence flows.
And, as the emotion deep and strong
Bears the wild crowd its path along,
The surging heart in every breast
Responsive sends a ringing shout,
Whose welcome din

Thro' all the music struggles in,
While to the echo pealeth out:
"Bravo! Il Maestro!
Mozart!
Mozart!!"
Cheer on cheer
The enraptured crowds prolong,
For the Shakespeare of the Realm of Tone,—
The Raphael of Song.
A few low chords,
Flute-like and clear,
Serve to give

Transition to the ear.
Very tender, very deep,
With burdened pathos
Are the strains that sweep
Surcharged with overflowing love,
That settles o'er the scene
Like a brooding dove.
E'en while the crowds
Move on their way,
The good, great heart
Seeks to impart
His pride and his joy in the strife,
To the faithful guardian of his life.
No words they speak;
Words are too weak
To paint emotion.
But, from the ocean
Of their love and pride,
A rising tide
Of heart communion flows.
The grey locks mingle with the auburn hair,
And there,
On his knees,
At his father's feet,

Their silent spirits meet.
And now,
Thro' gushing tears,
The Father kisses the Master's brow.

Falling like a heavy rain,
Drenching all the heart with pain,
A solemn, calm and gentle plaint
Throbs thro' the interlude.
Prolonged, sustained and slow
The varied harmonies flow,
Suggesting thro' the years they show,
An e'er increasing meed of woe;
Some heavy sorrow's weighty blow
Presaging to the troubled soul,
That human strength can not control.
A minor C.
"That key,
Sacred to tears,"
Arouses the fears.
While the plaint of the theme,
Like a chant in a dream,
Rises and swells, with solemn and dignified measure;

And the growing strains accumulate
  A thrilling, heavy and warning weight.
  The rich deep tones of a clarinet,
Where the waves of the melody have met,
        In notes of awful warning,
  And the pealing voice of the trumpet call,
  That starts, and wakens, and summons all
    To the Throne, at the Judgment morning,
  Gleam and crash thro' the sounding tide,
  And startle the chords they float beside,
    Then, sink in terrified silence.
  'Tis the "Dies Irae" of a Requiem Mass
  That flings its terrors on every class,
    And hovers in gloomy, sad portent,
    Wherever its thrilling notes are sent.
        And anguished souls,
        Where its warning rolls,
  Are almost o'erwhelmed by its billows.
        Until, at length,
    The tumult and the horror die
    In trembling supplication.
  And thro' the sweet strong concord fly
  The hopes of pardon and consolation;
    And the rising climax of the melody

Bursts forth in a glad "Benedictus."
Like mist to the rain,
Like sadness to pain,
Is the sorrow the music expresses,
Whose blending of gladness,
Along with the sadness,
Triumph and strength confesses.
A soft refrain, like distant bells,
Ringing their chimes with tender knells,
Steals o'er the sense
From the vault immense:
Till the waves of Eternity, receding far,
Come over the limit of Time's great bar,
Close to the weary heart of man,
Till he scarcely knows, if his brow be cooled
By the evening breeze of this life fair,
Or the Future's fresh, sweet morning air.

The light of the music is burning low,
And it falls like a halo, in golden glow,
Around a sorrowing little group,
Who sing thro' their tears such exquisite strain,
That angels, to hear its pathetic refrain,

From the heavenly radiance stoop.
"Requiem eternam eis," sings
The Master and his friends:
"'Tis for myself, said I not so?
    With it my life work ends."
The tender "Lachrymosa" brings
The loosened hold of his great heart's strings,
    And he weeps great tears,
The costly vintage of burdened years.
    'Tis sweet to live, but better to be
In the realms of bright Immortality,
    Where ever and ever, the soul shall find
The answering chords, that e'en here, bind
        The spirit to its God.
    When human effort attains the Best,
    What is left but eternal Rest,—
    Rest, where imperishable Beauty, forsooth,
    Rejoices in the freedom of Genius and Truth!
        He enters this Rest.
    Out from the beautiful courts above
    "Il Maestro" rings, with a peal of love
        Thro' the heavenly dome,
    As the seraphs lead his spirit home.

The light of the music gleams again,
In saddened mournful cadence,—when,
Out in the storm, not a single friend,
To do him honor, his presence doth lend,
Or mark the lonely grave.
" So great, so loved, so glorious,
So forgotten, so unrepaid."
A grave without a name!
And is this Fame?
For this the toil,
The aching brow, the heart's wild pain?
Well,—is it better on earth to learn
To live for a tomb with a golden urn?
Or to walk with God, and be no more,
Or from Nebo's height view the beautiful shore
Of the promised land?
Nay, *this* is Fame,—
A deathless name
Among the immortal band.
See! In Germany's musical heavens afar
He shines out clear their Morning Star,—
While Music hastens with honor meet
To lay her crown at the master's feet.
Aye, *this is Fame!*

Adown the surging galaxy of years,
Fame's herald bold,
With his trump of gold,
And brow among the stars,
Along the music's burning bars
Wings his triumphant course,—
A *Century* away,
From that weary day;—
And peals a note
From the golden throat,
Out, out to the coming years:
"Hail, Il Maestro!
Hail, thou Great Heart!
Hail, King of Tones!
All hail! Mozart!"

*　　*　　*　　*　　*　　*

"Requiem eternam ei, Domine,"
The music dies away
In faint far-echoed lay.
And, out from the Temple door,
That turns as noiseless as before,

The soul goes back
To the beaten track,
Of the duty allotted by God.
But, not as before
Is the heart so sore,
Nor the burden so weary and hard;
For the master of music,
And the Master above,
Have spoken a peace to the heart.
And we thank His Name
For Music's sweet spell,
And we whisper for courage
" Mozart ! "

www.ingramcontent.com/pod-product-compliance
Lightning Source LLC
Chambersburg PA
CBHW032117080426
42733CB00008B/966